ON THE AIR

ON THE AIR
BEHIND THE SCENES AT A TV NEWSCAST

Esther Hautzig   Photographs by **David Hautzig**

Macmillan Publishing Company   New York
Maxwell Macmillan Canada   Toronto
Maxwell Macmillan International   New York   Oxford   Singapore   Sydney

*With respect, gratitude, and affection for
everyone at WRGB-TV*
—E.H.

*I dedicate my half of this book to my father,
and to my mother (the other half of this book)*
—D.H.

Text copyright © 1991 by Esther Hautzig
Photographs copyright © 1991 by David Hautzig
Macmillan Publishing Company   Maxwell Macmillan Canada, Inc.
866 Third Avenue   1200 Eglinton Avenue East
New York, NY 10022   Suite 200
                                  Don Mills, Ontario M3C 3N1

First edition
Printed in the United States of America
10   9   8   7   6   5   4   3   2   1

The text of this book is set in 13 pt. Meridien
Book design by Christy Hale

Library of Congress Cataloging-in-Publication Data
Hautzig, Esther Rudomin.
On the air : behind the scenes at a TV newscast / by Esther Hautzig ;
    photographs by David Hautzig. — 1st ed.
        p.   cm.
Summary: Depicts how a typical television news broadcast is planned, put
    together, and presented.
ISBN 0-02-743361-7
1. Television broadcasting of news—Juvenile literature.   2. Reporters
and reporting—Juvenile literature.   [1. Television broadcasting of
news.   2. Reporters and reporting.]   I. Hautzig, David R., ill.
II. Title.
PN4784.T4H38   1991   070.1'95—dc20   91-6407

Wanting to know what's new in faraway places and where we live is as old as the world.

For centuries couriers on foot, birds carrying messages in their beaks, drumbeats, and smoke signals brought news from one community to another. More recently, news has been spread through newspapers, telegraphs, the Morse code, telephones, radio, and films.

Now television brings news into our daily lives. We see space shuttles going up, wars being fought, world series games being played, good news and bad right in our homes.

A broadcasting miracle occured on January 13, 1928, when Dr. E. F. W. Alexanderson, a researcher at General Electric, made the first public television broadcast from his home to the homes of four GE executives in Schenectady, New York. *The Boston Post* covered the story on their front page.

The first tv station, then called W2XB, was also founded in Schenectady in 1928. Television journalism started at that station. People now began to see news on the air, not only to read it in the newspapers and hear it on the radio. Kolin Hager became the country's first newscaster on May 10, 1928, when he began a farm and weather news program on W2XB.

W2XB also broadcast the first remote tv news, which was transmitted from one city to another.

The station was renamed WRGB-TV in 1942. The call letters are the initials of a real person: Dr. William R. G. Baker, a pioneer in the development of radio and tv at G.E. (General Electric).

WRGB-TV showed the first 15-minute, national newscast with Douglas Edwards in April 1948 which was, and still is, called national news. It is broadcast by networks to their affiliate stations all over the country. This book describes how a local newscast gets on the air.

Ernie Tetrault, the longest-tenured news anchor in the nation, began broadcasting local news over WRGB-TV in Schenectady in 1951. I've watched Ernie since 1960, so it is a special joy that WRGB-TV agreed to be part of this book. While other stations use somewhat different systems and equipment, or have more or fewer people on their staffs, this is how news gets on the air at WRGB.

The main WRGB studio is located in Schenectady, but it also has a news bureau and studio in Albany. It is widely known as NewsCenter 6 in the Albany / Schenectady / Troy area, and in several neighboring states. The Albany division of WRGB is called NewsCenter 6 / Capital Bureau.

WRGB-TV is an affiliate of the CBS Television Network. That means it receives all CBS network programs every day, as well as daily "feeds" of national and regional news. WRGB-TV anchors also cover international and national news in person. Ernie went to the Middle East during one of its strife-ridden periods and broadcast daily reports via satellite.

In addition, NewsCenter 6 broadcasts two and one-half hours of local news: thirty minutes at 6:30 in the morning, thirty minutes at noon, sixty minutes from 6:00 to 7:00 in the evening, and thirty minutes at 11:00 at night. WRGB-TV also broadcasts all special news programs from the CBS network, as well as the Evening News with the CBS national news anchor at 7:00 p.m.

TV technology transmits to us information from all over the world in a matter of minutes. But it is the dedicated men and women at tv stations who help us become enriched by its wonders.

This is the newsroom. At first glance it seems like an office where people work at desks with computers, telephones, and word processors. All these people are responsible for what we see on NewsCenter 6.

Gary Whitaker is the news director. Gary decides what will be shown on the newscasts. His office overlooks the newsroom and his door is always open. He questions and suggests, and cares about what goes on. He attends meetings with the management of WRGB-TV and with community leaders. He listens to their ideas of what news might be important to viewers in the area.

Neil Goldstein is the managing editor of NewsCenter 6. Neil is involved in each news segment. He decides which local events should be covered. He monitors computer screens, telephones news sources, and reads many newspapers and magazines. Neil writes *news breaks* and *news teasers* which highlight that day's news and are read throughout in the day on tv and radio. He edits news scripts to make them clearer and shorter. Each word, each second matters in a newscast.

Ernie Tetrault and Tracy Egan are the co-anchors of the nightly 6:00 p.m. and 11:00 p.m. newscasts. Although Ernie has broadcast news on WRGB-TV for more than forty years, he finds it as exciting today as he did when he started. Ernie says that his best local stories come through people he knows.

Tracy compares being an anchor to being a newspaper editor. As a reporter at several tv stations, she concentrated on only one story in a newscast. Now she enjoys being involved in all of them. Tracy is also the health editor of News-Center 6.

Liz Bishop anchors the *NewsCenter 6 at Noon* as well as the *NewsCenter 6:30 News*. She started at WRGB-TV as a sports reporter while she was in college. She is also the environmental news editor. *NewsCenter 6 at Noon* has features of interest to the community: interviews with local leaders and celebrities, financial reports, and entertainment news. The 6:30 p.m. news covers local and national stories.

Like other members of the news team, Liz broadcasts *news breaks* right from the newsroom. She reads 10- to 20-second news updates that will be reported in detail on the next newscast.

Mary Beth Wenger, who is both a reporter and the weekend anchor, decided to become a broadcaster when she was in the seventh grade. She loves being the first to tell people what's new: "It's like being the town crier." Mary Beth says she has the best of all possible worlds—two days of anchoring news and three days of reporting and writing her own news segments. Human-interest stories are those she cares about most.

Jack Aernecke anchors the *NewsCenter 6 First News* at 6:30 a.m. on weekdays and reports financial news on the noon and 6:30 p.m. newscasts almost every day. Jack does other news stories at WRGB as well. Everyone at the station is both a specialist and a skilled general reporter of news of the day.

Mary Ballou is assistant to the news director, an associate producer at the station, director of special services, and coordinator of community programs. She's worked behind the scenes at WRGB-TV for over fifteen years. Mary's day begins at 5:30 a.m. when she comes to the newsroom, looks over reports which came in during the night, and makes calls to see what's happening. She co-produces *NewsCenter 6 Sunday Morning News* and a weekly program called *Student Spectrum* on which young people discuss issues that interest them.

There are many other newscasters at WRGB. Just count the names when credits roll by at the end of a newscast on *your* tv!

Approximately 75 percent of all national and international news comes to WRGB-TV from the Associated Press wire service and CBS network. WRGB pays a yearly fee to AP which has hundreds of news bureaus and thousands of reporters all over the world. Buttons called "routers" are posted near desks. They list numbers to be punched in on computers when a reporter or producer wants to check out a news item. Another button will activate the printer to print out the news story on paper.

WRGB-TV also gets news from satellites. Satellites are positioned in space, 22,300 miles above the earth. They are used to relay both pictures and sound from one place to another all over the world. The station has a satellite truck with a miniature control room inside it. It can relay video and sound from anywhere in the country. WRBG satellite dishes are set up in back of the station and on top of the roof to receive signals.

The tape room is a giant supply store of video information on many subjects. Router boxes are attached to television monitors throughout NewsCenter 6 and have numbers for every tape source in the tape room. People can choose what they want to watch by pushing the right button. Videotapes from satellites are stored on one-inch tape.

Scanners provide information about local events. They work on special air frequencies and monitor police and fire departments. If there's a fire, burglary, or crime, everyone in the newsroom knows about it immediately. Newscasters also have scanners and two-way radios in their cars.

The WRGB-TV Tips Phone rings all day and all night with news from people who live in the area. Gary Whitaker and Neil Goldstein decided one day to follow up on a story of a badly abused kitten. When viewers asked why so much attention was spent on an abused animal, Gary and Neil said on the weekly *Sunday News Program*: "We want the public to know that people who can do what they did to this kitten may do it to human beings as well."

The five weekday and four weekend newscasts at WRGB-TV have different producers. Each producer monitors news from the Associated Press, the CBS network, and satellite transmissions. They read newspapers and magazines and listen to the scanners and WRGB-TV Tips Phone reports. Every producer attends meetings with the news director, managing editor, reporters, and assignment editors. They make important decisions with the anchors and with directors who are in charge of the actual broadcasts. As one of them said, "We're in this together."

Producers are in charge of the content and write most of each newscast script. Since every second is crucial, their computers are programmed to count airtime. The speed with which Ernie and Tracy speak has also been programmed into computers.

After everyone is satisfied with the script, it goes into a special printing machine. Words that are read on air by a reporter or anchor are printed in capital letters. Prerecorded text is in upper- and lowercase letters. The printing machine magnifies each letter as it comes in from the word processor. (It is later magnified again in the TelePrompTer machine.) Each line has four or fewer words and takes one second to read. This makes it easy to check how long it'll take to read a story.

Each story is printed on six layers of different colored paper. The white copy goes to the TelePrompTer operator, pink and blue to the anchors, green to the audio control operator, yellow to the director, and gold to the producer. The pages are separated into six piles by whoever has time to lend a hand.

Pictures accompanying news stories are called *graphics*. A character generator, which looks like a huge typewriter, produces all kinds of graphics. An electronic surface is positioned next to the keyboard. The graphic designer uses a special pen, called a stylus, to create a picture which appears on one of the monitors. The designer can adjust the picture, choosing different colors, letters, and special effects by pushing different buttons. Graphic designs are preprogrammed and stored on computer floppy disks for use during newscasts. A printed schedule of graphics is given to everyone involved in a newscast.

The editorial meeting, which is the most important meeting of the day for newsroom people, takes place each morning at about 9:00. Gary Whitaker, Neil Goldstein, producers, reporters, graphic designers, anchors, and the assignment editor get together to go over the agenda for that day's newscasts. This involves discussion and many decisions. A thirty-minute newscast includes only twenty-four minutes of news. The rest is taken by commercials.

Polls show that people prefer human-interest stories and news of their communities to stories of faraway places. But what if there's news about trouble in a place from which we import oil, sugar, or coffee? That will affect everyone who lives in the NewsCenter 6 viewing area. It must be included on the 6:00 news. How about a story of senior citizens' feelings about aging and where they can get help?

Everyone agreed at one editorial meeting to do such a feature story. Larry Schwartz, the assignment editor, decided to give this story to Ken Screvin who works in the NewsCenter 6/Capital Bureau in Albany. Ken had just walked in from another assignment and didn't have time to take off his coat.

A feature like this, also called a package, takes hours to prepare and just a few minutes to present. Larry called the senior citizens' center. Ken called Help Line which older people call when they need help. Both the senior citizens' center and the director of Help Line gave Larry and Ken permission to do the story. Before leaving the meeting, Ken talked to a producer and to his camera operator, Ed Curley, about it.

First, Ken and Ed went to the senior citizens' center. Before they began to interview people, they checked their equipment.

First Ken spoke to people who work at the center while Ed videotaped their conversations. Ken later interviewed several senior citizens individually to get their own points of view. A good reporter like Ken talks to a lot of people when doing a news report.

When Ed and Ken finished at the senior citizens' center, they went to the office of Help Line. They met the director of Help Line who told Ken about the kind of help senior citizens need. Next Ed and Ken went inside to speak to the volunteer who directs callers to the best sources of help. Sometimes the callers just want someone to talk to because they are lonely.

After Ken interviewed everyone, he did a *stand up*. This appears at the end of a news feature and lasts about 20 seconds. It presents additional facts, sums up what everyone said or highlights something especially meaningful.

After Ken and Ed taped everything they wanted, they went back to the WRGB Albany studio. Ken put the tape in a video-tape machine and timed how long each picture lasted on the screen. This is called *logging a tape.* For example, Ed videotaped the outside of the senior citizens' center for 30 seconds, so Ken wrote down that time segment on a pad of paper. He also listened and timed and wrote down what people said and how long each "scene" lasted. Ed had to make choices and logging the tape made it easier. He consulted with Larry, Neil, and his producer as he worked.

When Ken wrote the script for his news story, he also chose and timed which parts of the videotape and interviews he was

going to use. He then recorded the *voice-over* for the story in the audio room: His voice will relate the story on the newscast while the videotape is played.

Finally, Ed and Ken edited the videotape so that it would take the exact number of minutes and seconds allotted for playing it on the newscast.

When all the work on the news story was done, Ken watched it again to make sure that he was satisfied. Afterward the tape was sent by microwave transmission from Albany to the station in Schenectady. This means that while the tape was being played in Albany, the sound and picture were transmitted on special radio frequencies. They were "caught" by two antennas

on the roof of WRGB-TV and recorded on a videocassette in the tape room. The tape was played later that day on a newscast and was watched in many homes.

Some of the interviews Liz Bishop conducts are shown through a process called *chroma keying*. "Chroma" means color and "keying" means inserting a live image over another video source. It is an electronic special-effects system which combines two pictures in separate locations and shows them together on the tv screen.

One day Liz interviewed Mirinda, a young country music singer who was at home while Liz was in the studio.

A remote truck was sent to Mirinda's house. The video and the sound of Mirinda's voice went from her house to the truck through wires. Then the remote truck sent both by microwave transmission to WRGB to be picked up by the roof antennas and shown on television.

While the picture of Mirinda could be seen on tv, Liz was looking at a blank screen painted bright green. A chroma-key screen is usually bright green or a special shade of blue. Blue or green is used because there is no blue or green in the skin colors of people. Keying is a kind of hole: Whatever isn't blue or green will be seen against the screen. Whatever *is* blue or green will not show up against the screen—it will become transparent and blend into the background.

The chroma-key process permitted Mirinda's image to be superimposed on the green screen, for viewing on home tv screens and studio monitors but not on the studio screen itself. Newscasters like Liz are used to it; talking to a blank screen is sometimes part of the job.

"What's the weather tomorrow?"

John Cessarich, who received a degree in meteorology, which is the science dealing with atmosphere, weather, and climate, forecasts the weather on NewsCenter 6.

Every WRGB forecaster works in the weather center on the set. Electronic computer printouts of weather predictions and patterns for specific areas come from the National Meteorological Center every hour. He studies maps of atmospheric conditions, cloud formations, rainfall measurements, and other meteorological conditions.

The forecaster's most important tool is the radar screen which comes via satellite to a monitor on his table. The satellite picture of the earth shows him just what weather trends are in the making. He studies these trends, compares them with maps which are hung on his walls, and makes his predictions for the WRGB area. When mistakes in weather predictions occur, we're upset with the weather forecaster. However, nature can be unpredictable despite the best calculations and study.

"Who's winning?"

Everybody wants to know the scores for their favorite teams, whether the local basketball star is being recruited by Syracuse University, and which players are being traded.

When Mike Cairns, one of the sportscasters, comes to the newsroom, he first checks news services which provide that evening's sports lineups. He also looks in newspapers for the schedule of local high school football and basketball games.

There may be seven hockey games, five basketball games, a tennis tournament in France, a boxing match in Japan, and national ice skating championships—not to mention twenty or more local high school and college games. Mike has to report on all these events in less than five minutes.

Mike decides which national games he will videotape in the sportscasters' area of the newsroom. From these tapes he will choose exciting plays, called *hi-lites,* to show on the broadcast. If he cannot use what he has taped, Mike will pick up hi-lites provided by the CBS network and CNN. These are services to which the station subscribes and receives via satellite.

Since the producer and Mike know that people want to see local games, a camera person is sent to some high school games. Mike logs the tape on his VTR and chooses some hi-lites. He talks things over with the producer and finds out the exact number of minutes and seconds he'll have for sports on the newscast. After Mike makes final hi-lite choices, he times them, writes down the numbers where they appear on the videotape, and takes his script and videotape to an editor in the editing room.

NewsCenter 6 in Schenectady has five editing booths. Anchors, reporters, producers, and editors use them constantly. Everyone logs his or her tape, just as Ken did in the Capitol Bureau studio and Mike did at his desk in the newsroom. They choose material from tapes for their news story and almost always turn it over to an editor to put it together.

Each editing booth consists of two VTRs and monitors. The reporter feeds tape of the news story into one VTR, called the *source*, and plays it back in sequence. After the most interesting parts of the news story have been chosen, the reporter writes down the numbers which indicate where they are on the tape and how long they last.

The editor then takes over the job and puts it together in the second VTR. This is called the *record VTR*—it performs actual edits electronically. The editor doesn't decide what is used. She or he only combines, trims, and matches the videotape to the exact number of seconds alloted to a news story.

When a producer, anchor, or reporter wants to include material from a previous newscast in a current news story, an intern gets the right videotape from the WRGB-TV library.

The tape library has thousands of old films and tapes of newscasts, just as this year's and next year's news will be there decades from now.

The final tapes are turned over to the tape-room operator. During a broadcast each of the tapes will be part of the news, but few viewers realize how many skilled people and which complicated machines put it all together.

The control room is the brain of the newscast. Its power to do so much at the push of buttons can seem awesome. But the buttons don't push themselves and they don't make decisions. People make decisions and direct machines to follow their orders.

The person who makes the most important decisions during the newscast is the director. The director consults the producer before airtime. They discuss the script, the sequence of stories, and delays that may occur in getting videotapes for the broadcast.

The director acts like a "translator" between the newscasters and the technical crew. He gives cues in a language that's clear only to people who work together in broadcasting. He coordinates the work of camera people, audio engineers, graphic machine operators. He listens to the producer, the floor man-

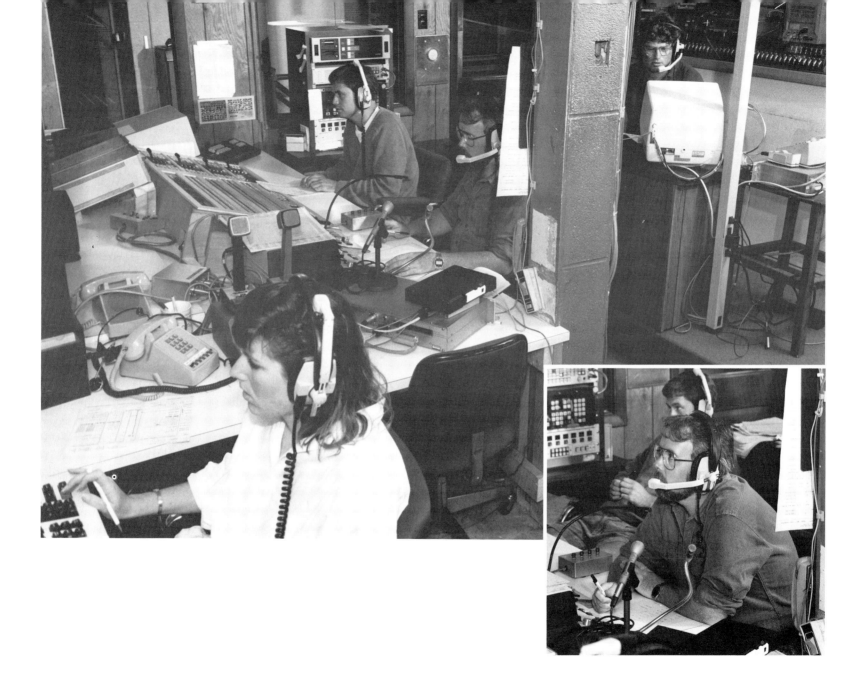

ager, the master control engineers. He looks at monitors that show what each camera is seeing, and he checks a stopwatch and the control room clock for running time on individual news segments.

The director sits next to the technical director, known as the T.D., who operates the video switcher. Everything that's shown during a newscast is plugged into the switcher. The switcher has separate buttons for each camera, videotape, and remote inputs. There are buttons which control background color, graphics, special effects, and many other very technical functions. The T.D. understands the director's language of very fast cues and transfers them to the switcher keyboard.

The T.D. looks like a pianist, playing newscast sources instead of music. It seems impossible that he or she can push all the buttons as quickly as the director gives the cues. However, the T.D. does it as effortlessly as a performer who has memorized the music.

The audio control booth is a small, separate room with a large glass window overlooking the control room. The walls are padded with a special foam to make it soundproof and quiet. The audio control board looks like a video switcher, but it controls only sound.

The audio engineer does not hear the noise in the control room. He hears only the director's cues through an intercom. The audio engineer checks the volume meter. He makes sure

that all the microphones work well in the studio, that the videotapes, remote location transmissions, the musical themes and commericals have good sound. The audio control room is the most peaceful place during a newscast.

The graphics operator in the control room is in charge of the graphics which were designed in the newsroom and put on a disk. When the director gives a cue, the graphics operator makes it available to the T.D.

Steve St. George, the tape operator, is an important member of the control room team. When the director gives a cue to play Ken's tape on senior citizens, Steve puts it in the videotape player. As soon as the first image comes up on the monitor, he stops. It's then ready for the T.D. After the tape is played, Steve takes it out and on the director's cue, puts in the next tape. During a thirty-minute newscast, he will handle about thirty-five different tapes.

Since the producer's overall responsibility is the content of each newscast, he sits in the control room right behind the director and the T.D. Quite often the producer has to make important decisions while the news is being broadcast.

For example, before going on air he had timed the newscast to the exact second: Ken's story on senior citizens is two minutes and ten seconds, sports is three minutes and forty seconds, weather gets two minutes and ten seconds, etc. But if anyone makes their story longer by even twenty seconds while broadcasting it, the producer has a problem.

The producer has to look ahead at the script on the computer and quickly decide where he can cut those twenty seconds. He may tell Mike to shorten his sports news, or he may cut out an entire twenty-second story. Since the script is printed in four-word, one-second lines, the producer knows just how many lines have to be cut to save twenty seconds.

The producer tells the director what cuts to make and the director then informs everyone in the control room and the studio. Everyone who has a script quickly finds the material and takes it out. Newscasting can be very nerve-racking!

Master control is the pulse of the station. It's like the beat a conductor gives to an orchestra which musicians and instruments must follow. It controls everything: network shows, local programs, commercials, public service announcements, station breaks. It makes sure that every show is broadcast at the right time. To the second.

The master control engineer makes sure that this happens. He is also responsible for the technical quality of all the programs on WRGB-TV.

At about 4:30 in the afternoon, Ernie and Tracy begin to get ready for the 6:00 Evening News and Liz for the 6:30 news program. It's hard to think of newscasters having makeup put on their faces, and it isn't done to make them look glamorous.

But what's the first thing you look at when you adjust the color on your tv? A face on the screen. A makeup expert comes in the afternoon to make sure that the anchors' skin tones look natural under studio lights, that minor scratches or mosquito bites are hidden, that lipstick colors on women will reproduce well on television.

After that's done, the anchors go back to the newsroom and get ready to do the NewsCenter 6 Evening News.

While Ernie, Tracy, and Liz prepare in the newsroom, the people in the studio get ready for their duties during the broadcast.

The WRGB-TV studio was built in 1957. It is the nation's first studio designed especially for color tv broadcasts. The ceilings are high, so that the lights are far up and not too hot for anchors, camera operators, and others in the studio. The lighting board was installed when the studio was built and has been preset for newscasts for many years.

The floor is perfectly level so that cameras can roll smoothly and noiselessly from one place to another. It is also very strong so that the equipment can be moved without causing damage. The walls and ceiling are covered with special acoustical material. The studio has no windows to shut out noise and light interference.

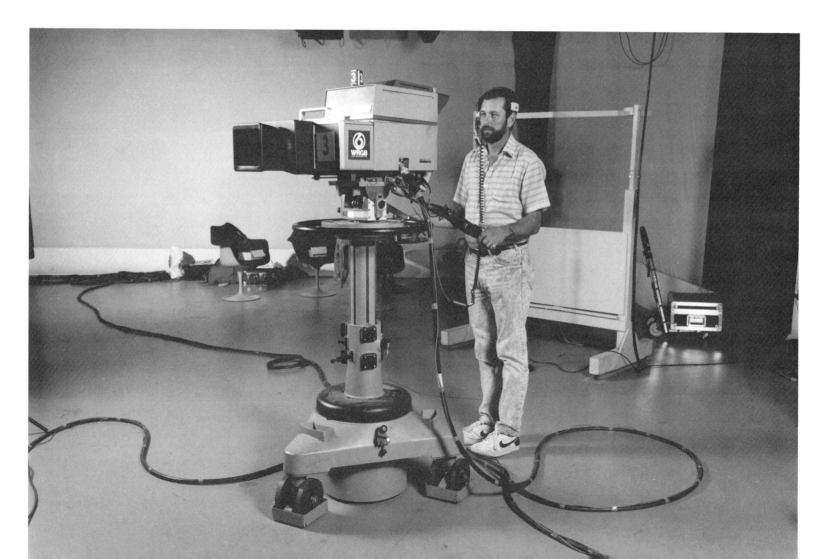

Three cameras film the newscast at WRGB-TV. They are massive and can be moved from place to place only on pedestals with wheels. They are operated on electrical current through many feet of very heavy cables. The most important features of each camera are the imaging device, the viewfinder, the filter, and the intercom system.

Before a newscast each camera operator puts on a headset and makes sure that the intercom system with the control room is functioning. They check the lens and make sure that the monitor attached to the camera is properly connected. During the newscast each camera operator must be in constant touch with the director, the T.D., and the video and audio engineers so that they can follow every cue instantly.

In addition to the camera people, there's a floor manager in the studio. Don Keenan wears headphones and relays instructions from the control room to everyone in the studio. He gives cues to communicate without words what must be done—he uses a "language of motions." For instance, the floor manager cues in an anchor which camera he should face. He gives time cues by holding up five, four, three, two, or one finger, "telling" newscasters how many seconds they have to finish their story. If they are too slow, he rotates his forefingers clockwise; if they are too fast, he motions with both hands as if he is stretching a huge rubber band.

Don also makes sure that cameras don't crash into each other since a camera operator looks only into his viewfinder. It's up to the floor manager to make things run smoothly in the studio.

Anchors and reporters do not memorize their scripts. They have a copy of the script on the set, but they read the text from a monitor called a *TelePrompTer* on each of the cameras. The TelePrompTer operator is important in making a newscast go smoothly. She moves the script on a surface that looks like a conveyor belt, past a camera which transmits the words to the monitors on each of the studio cameras. A mirror projects the text onto a glass plate right over the camera lens.

The anchors and reporters look directly into the camera and read the script. The TelePrompTer operator moves the script at the same pace as the anchors and reporters read them.

Mike Cairns, the sports reporter, prefers to read his script without a TelePrompTer. He thinks it looks more natural to read scores from a script on his desk. John Cessarich explains weather patterns and makes predictions in front of a map or chart also without a TelePrompTer.

The set from which news is broadcast has a monitor at each person's seat. The anchors and reporters can watch the monitors while the camera is not on them, or when taped material is shown during the news. There are telephones on the sides of the long desk in case anyone needs to make an urgent call.

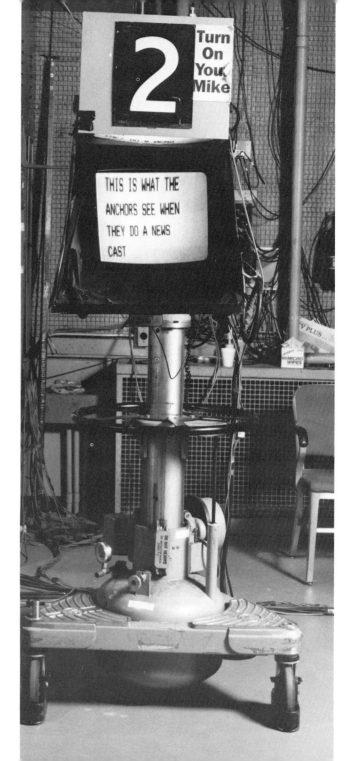

Excitement and tension build when Tracy and Ernie get down to the news set about fifteen minutes before they go on the air.

Like pilots in a cockpit, they check all their equipment. They test their microphones which are the size of the last joint of a little finger. The mike is attached to Tracy's jacket or blouse, and to Ernie's tie, about six inches below the chin. This seems to be just the right place for sound reproduction without any distortion.

The anchors and reporters wear nearly invisible earphones to stay in touch with the control room. They need to know when a late-breaking story comes over a satellite or AP wire, or whether a story has to be cut at the last minute.

After the final countdown, NewsCenter 6 Evening News goes on the air. The electronic wonders and satellites, the machines and cameras, mikes and monitors, control rooms and switches, remote trucks and wire transmissions are all ready to roll.

And yet, when you come right down to it, it is not only news of the world but *stories* that newscasters bring into our homes that seem to matter a lot. We care about senior citizens and watch reports such as Ken's with concern. We want to know about people and events in our communities. We cheer for high school basketball players and we root for local teams when they play on tv.

When the newscast is over, the broadcasters, camera people, technical staff, directors, producers, tape operators, editors, and interns sign off, but not for long. A new cycle of preparations for the next newscast begins almost immediately. It is only a few hours off.

Once more we'll be switching on the tv to hear,

''What's new?''